Short _ish_ Walks

on and around

The Lizard

Paul White

Bossiney Books

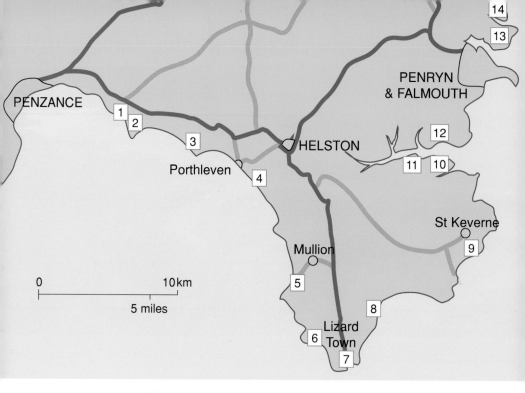

The approximate locations of the walks in this book

All the walks in this book were checked prior to this reprint, at which time the instructions were correct. However, changes can occur in the countryside over which neither the author nor publisher has any control. Please let us know if you encounter any serious problems.

This reprint 2016
First published 2010 by
Bossiney Books Ltd, 33 Queens Drive, Ilkley, LS29 9QW
www.bossineybooks.com

ISBN 978-1906474-25-6
Acknowledgements
The maps are by Nick Hawken
Cover based on a design by Heards Design Partnership
All photographs are by the author
The boots on the front cover were kindly supplied by the Brasher Boot Company
Printed in Great Britain by R Booth Ltd, Penryn, Cornwall

Introduction

A 'shortish' walk is typically 6-8 km (4-5 miles) in length, and likely to take 2-3 hours. How long you actually take will depend on your fitness, the weather conditions, and how much you find to interest you along the way.

All the walks are circular, involving a stretch of cliff path and an inland return. Eight are on the Lizard peninsula itself, with three along the coast to either side. Needless to say, the scenery varies from the delightful to the spectacular.

The walks may be shortish, but some of them can be quite tough going in places, especially on the cliff path. You will find strenuous ascents and descents, some uneven walking and quite a few stiles, some of them requiring agility. Proper walking boots are vital for grip and ankle support and a walking pole or stick is useful for balance in the descents. On the inland sections you may well find muddy patches even in dry weather, not to mention briars, thistles, gorse and nettles, so bare legs are a liability.

Safety – a real issue for walkers in this area

Cliff walking can be very exposed: the wind-chill factor is like being out in the Atlantic, and of course Cornish weather can change very rapidly, so you need extra layers of clothing, as well as waterproofs, for what is often an abrupt change of temperature between inland and cliff walking.

The most obvious hazard is the cliff path. It is not fenced off from the drop and in some of the walks passes quite near the edge. Walk no nearer the drop than you have to and keep a close eye on children and dogs. It is not safe to walk the cliffs in gale conditions, especially with children. This is no place for bravado. Make sure you take a supply of water with you: dehydration makes you tired.

The maps provided in this book look very attractive but they are only sketch maps, so you may well want to carry the OS 1:25000 map.

The Cornish countryside

Despite many pressures, Cornish farmers are still trying to make a living from the land you are passing through. Please respect crops, leave gates open or shut as you find them, and keep dogs under control when near livestock.

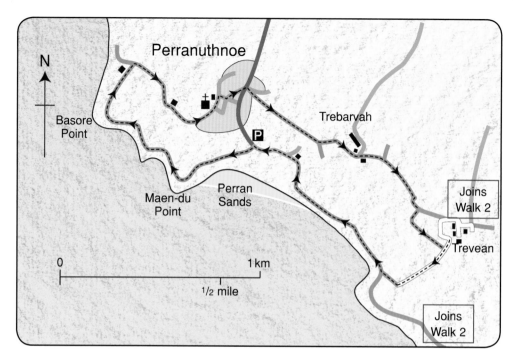

Walk 1 Perranuthnoe

Distance: 5km (3 miles)   Time: 1 1/2 hours
Character: A walk dominated by views over Mount's Bay and over
Perran Sands from the coast path, with an inland return by pleasant
paths and tracks. Easy walking. Can be combined with Walk 2.

Start from the main car park in Perranuthnoe, near Perran Sands beach (SW 540294). Take the path on the opposite side of the road, COAST PATH PUBLIC FOOTPATH MARAZION. Follow it round Basore Point, until it passes inland of a house. Just after leaving National Trust land, turn right at a T-junction on a track.

On reaching a lane, continue ahead past the church and the Church Room, then turn right down a street. Turn left at the crossroads and pass the Victoria Inn.

Cross over at the next junction and walk beside 'Churchway Cottage', then after 40m bear right on a PUBLIC FOOTPATH. At a path junction, keep left up the slope. Follow the well-beaten path round the edge of a field. Cross the yard at Trebarvah, keeping left then bearing right through a gate (PUBLIC FOOTPATH) and follow further signs.

Continue up a field with the hedge on your left and at the far end cross a stile. Turn right and keep the hedge on your right round two

4

sides of the field. Where the field path bears left, about 100 m before Trevean House, take the waymarked path on your right. After 50 m go through a kissing gate and turn left. When you reach a track, turn right and follow it towards the coast. When the track ends, turn right, towards St Michael's Mount.

On reaching the coast path (acorn signs) continue ahead (or turn sharp left to join Walk 2) and follow the acorn signs till you reach a tarmac lane and a house. Turn left on the lane, then bear left at the next junction, and you will arrive back at the car park.

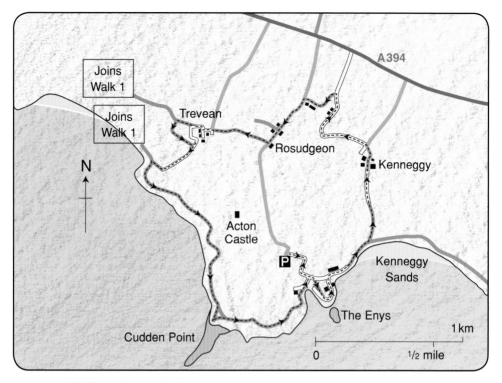

Walk 2   Prussia Cove

Distance: 6.7km (4¹/4 miles)   Time: 2¹/4 hours
Character: A delightfully varied walk, mixing magnificent coastal
scenery with inland paths. Prussia Cove was once the home of the
Carter brothers, Cornwall's most famous smugglers – Harry Carter
even wrote an autobiography in 1809. It is clear from this that
the brothers had at least one wealthy local backer – probably John
Stackhouse of Acton Castle. Can be combined with walk 1.

Park at the Prussia Cove's Porth-en-Alls car park (SW 556282). Leave
by the vehicle entrance and immediately turn right. Follow a gravel
track, which winds down to a junction. Bear left, then turn right down
a narrow footpath.

After 100m join a track following the windings of the shoreline
eastward. After passing an old quarry the track becomes a path, and
there is soon a fork, above Kenneggy Sands.

Bear left, steeply uphill (KENNEGGY). The path becomes a track,
then a tarmac lane. After another 125m, beside the entrance to Sunny
Vale Farm, turn left down an old track. Keep right when the track
opens out into a triangular area. After passing some unusual eco-

friendly buildings, turn sharp left at a path junction. This leads past more conventional buildings to a lane. Turn left and follow the lane for 300m, crossing a small valley.

Opposite Rosudgeon Farm turn right on PUBLIC FOOTPATH. Cross a stile and continue with the hedge on your left. Cross another stile and continue with the hedge on your right.

On reaching Trevean Farm, cross the tarmac track and continue ahead to 'Trevean House'. Continue on the track to the right, and keep the hedge on your left for 100m. Then turn left (waymarked) and after 50m go through a kissing gate and turn left. Notice Acton Castle ahead of you. On reaching a track, turn right along it towards the coast.

When the track ends, turn right, towards Perran Sands and St Michael's Mount. (People have made an unofficial path down the field ahead, but this is not an official right of way.) On reaching the coast path, turn sharp left (or continue ahead to join Walk 1) and follow it southward to Cudden Point, then eastward until you reach a thatched cottage. Bear left up a few steps, and turn right onto a track.

Continue ahead at the first track junction, then at a fork keep left, and follow the track back up to the car park.

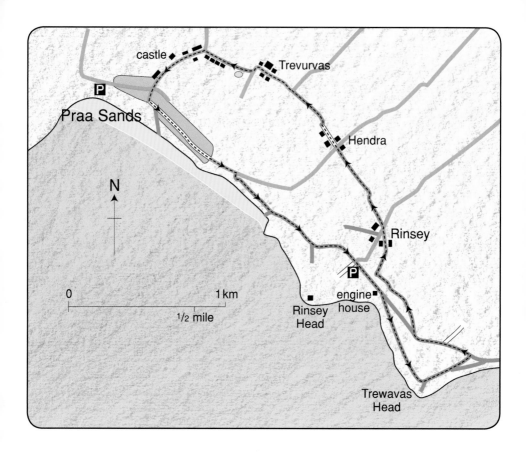

Walk 3 Rinsey and Pengersick

Distance: 6.75 km (4¹/₄ miles)   Time: 2 hours
Character: Stunning coastline scenery, with a pleasant inland stretch
through farmland. Fairly easy walking with gentle ascents and
descents.

Start from the National Trust car park at Rinsey (SW 592271). (You could, alternatively, start from Praa Sands.)

Walk down past the engine house and bear right down the coast path (acorn sign). It crosses the neck of Trewavas Head, then passes a strange natural sculpture. At a path junction continue ahead (acorn sign) then at a T-junction turn left.

At the top of the slope you will be faced with three gates. Cross the stile beside the gate on the left. Keep right when the path forks, which takes you above the engine house, then turns inland to Rinsey.

Join a tarmac lane. Ignore the road junction on the left and the

first footpath on your left, then after 50 m turn left through a kissing gate (PUBLIC FOOTPATH). Turn left through another kissing gate, then keep the hedge on your right, following yellow waymarks to the next hamlet, Hendra.

Turn right onto a lane, then after 30 m left (PUBLIC FOOTPATH), passing 'Mount's Bay View'. Cross a stile on the right and follow the path to a lane. Turn left and walk through the hamlet of Trevurvas, following the lane round to the left, then branching right on a PUBLIC BRIDLEWAY. A grassy path soon brings you to a street of bungalows.

At the T-junction turn left and walk on the pavement past Pengersick Castle. After a row of shops, continue ahead at the cross-roads (UNSUITABLE FOR CARAVANS) then turn left (GREENWAYS) into what soon becomes a track.

It would be very understandable if you preferred at this point to make your way down to the beach and turn left along it. Otherwise, continue along the track past a range of holiday homes. The track becomes a lane. When it bears left and starts to head uphill, turn right then immediately left (COAST PATH).

Keep following signs for the coast(al) path and it will take you inland of the dramatically positioned house on Rinsey Head and back to the Rinsey car park.

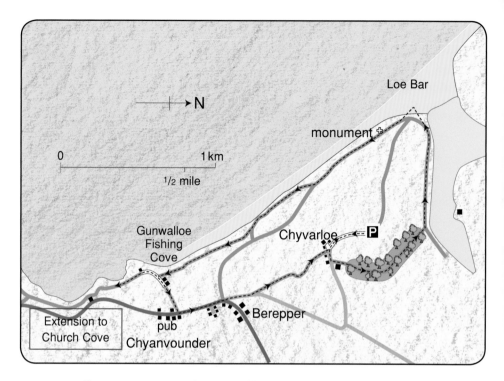

Walk 4   Loe Bar and Gunwalloe

Distance: 6km (3³/4 miles) or 10.4km (6¹/2 miles)
Time: 1¹/2 hours or 3 hours
*Character: The basic circuit is easy walking, though the cliff path goes
disconcertingly near the edge, so it's not one for vertigo sufferers: it
includes fields, woodland, Loe Bar (a natural shingle bar blocking a river
outlet) and a long stretch of cliff path. The extension to Church Cove
adds some more dramatic cliff scenery and one of Cornwall's loveliest
sandy beaches, with its very own church and separate bell-tower.
NB Loe Bar is a notoriously dangerous beach for swimming.*

Start from the National Trust car park at Chyvarloe – to get there,
within Gunwalloe turn right at a T-junction (LOOE BAR HELSTON).
Take the first left, signed LOOE BAR SANDS, and then continue on a
rough track signed CAR PARK.

Walk back along the track. Just before barns on your left, and opposite 'Chyvarloe Wartha', turn left onto a footpath. Cross the stile, go
through a gate and descend to another gate into woodland. On the
far side of the wood go through two field gates then turn left onto the
path beside Carminoe Creek. This leads out to Loe Bar.

Walk out onto the bar, then turn left. Take the right-hand path, passing the memorial to the crew of HMS *Anson*.

Bear right at an acorn waymark. Continue along the narrow cliff path, keeping clear of the crumbly edge and following any diversions. You will arrive at Gunwalloe Fishing Cove*. Turn left up a track which soon becomes a narrow lane. At the T-junction, you may be tempted by the Halzephron Inn a little to the right. Otherwise turn left and continue along the lane to a lane junction.

Take the minor lane ahead (LOOE BAR HELSTON). After 230 m turn left, PUBLIC FOOTPATH. Cross several small fields with stiles, then turn right into a grassy track which leads back to Chyvarloe. Turn right then sharp left, back to the car park.

The extension to Church Cove
*From Fishing Cove, continue along a track, which becomes a path at 'Parc Bean'. Follow it up to a lane and turn right on the path, at first parallel to the lane then bearing away to the right around Halzephron Cliff. Follow the coast path round to Church Cove, where there is a café as well as toilets. This is deservedly a popular family beach. In high season you may want to return by way of the cliffs at least as far as Halzephron House, but at other times you could walk back up the lane which is a shorter route.

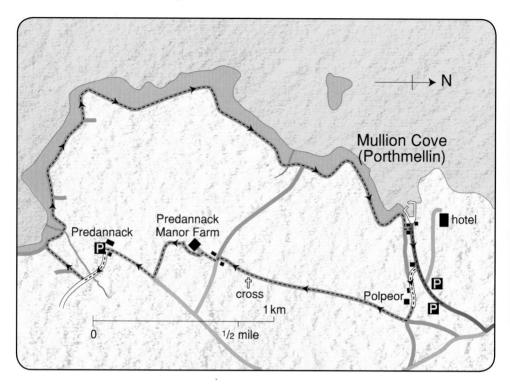

Walk 5   Mullion Cove and Predannack

Distance: 7km (4 1/2 miles)   Time: 2 hours
*Character: Pleasant field paths and a nature reserve on the inland
stretch, then cliff path with views getting better and better. Ascents and
descents with uneven walking and some difficult stiles. Can be quite
muddy in places.*

Approach Mullion Cove (a.k.a. Porthmellin) from Mullion village and
park at one of the two car parks. Walk a further 100m down the lane
from the lower car park, then turn sharp left on a track past Mullion
Cove Lodges which leads uphill.

   Ignore the first footpath to the right and continue up past Polpeor
to a waymarked path crossing. Turn right across a stile and keep the
hedge on your left.

   The path goes through the Lizard Nature Reserve then across more
fields, past a medieval cross, to a group of houses. Continue ahead
on a lane, but turn left (PUBLIC FOOTPATH) just before Predannack
Manor Farm. Keep the hedge on your right, then cross a stile on the
right. A well-trodden path to your left leads across fields out to a lane.

Turn right. The lane ends at the National Trust car park at Predannack: turn left between buildings (COAST PATH) onto a track. Cross a stream then turn right (COAST PATH).

Turn right when you reach the coast path, and simply follow it for 3.5 km to Mullion Cove. Descend to the harbour, turn briefly left then right up the lane back to the car park.

The Lizard National Nature Reserve

This consists of 2000 hectares managed by Natural England, but comprising at least six separate locations. The Mullion and Predannack Cliffs reserve is home to a wide variety of wild flowers, including squill, wild chives and green-winged orchids. And where there is interesting vegetation, there is usually interesting bird and insect life too. The cliffs were in the past used for communal grazing, but this has declined commercially: Natural England, and in other parts of the cliffs the National Trust, organise seasonal grazing by Soay sheep and Shetland ponies to prevent woody shrubs taking over from the wild flowers. The inland footpath through the reserve is quite enclosed, so don't expect to see too much on that stretch.

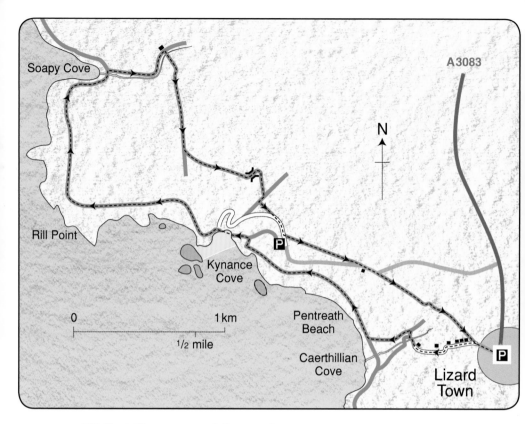

Walk 6 Kynance and Soapy Cove

Distance: 9km (5 1/2 miles)   Time: 2 1/2 hours
Alternatively, for a 5km walk start from the National Trust car park rather than from Lizard Town.
Character: A walk to show the massive contrasts of the Lizard –
outward past some of the Cornish coast's most dramatic scenery, with steep ascents and descents, then easy walking back across the Lizard's heathland – pleasant enough, and a paradise for botanists and entomologists, but so featureless that I don't recommend coming back this way without a compass if it's foggy!

Start from Lizard Town's central car park (donations). Head westward on the No Through Road signed TO CAERTHILLIAN AND KYNANCE COVES and continue along the rough lane past houses. It ultimately becomes a footpath, leading down into the valley. Cross a tiny brook then turn sharp right. Go through a gate, then turn left at a T junction. Follow this path out to join the coast path, and turn right.

14

Follow the coast path past the National Trust car park and down to cross the beach, pass the café and turn left to continue on the coast path. Even on an August Bank Holiday, the steep slope ahead soon thins out the crowds! The views become ever more dramatic. The path rounds Rill Point, and new views open up across Mount's Bay.

The next major inlet is Gew Graze, better known as Soapy Cove, from the white 'soaprock' or steatite which is seen in the cliffs opposite. It is a form of talc and was quarried at Soapy Cove from the late 18th century to the 1840s by the Worcester firm of Flight & Barr for use in the manufacture of porcelain.

Turn right along the cliff and descend into the valley. Cross the stream and turn right up a track. After passing houses above you on the left, turn sharp right across a ford. A well-made track leads up to and through an English Nature reserve.

At the far end, take the left gate out of three (PERMISSIVE BRIDLEWAY) and bear left along the broad grassy track towards Lizard Town in the distance. Follow the waymarks. Cross a footbridge and climb a slope. On reaching a broad sandy track, turn right, then shortly left on a path towards the car park. Reaching a gravel track, turn left.

Opposite the pedestrian entrance to the car park, turn left on a path through the heather. Join a lane for 100m then continue ahead, PUBLIC FOOTPATH. This well trodden path leads you back to Lizard Town.

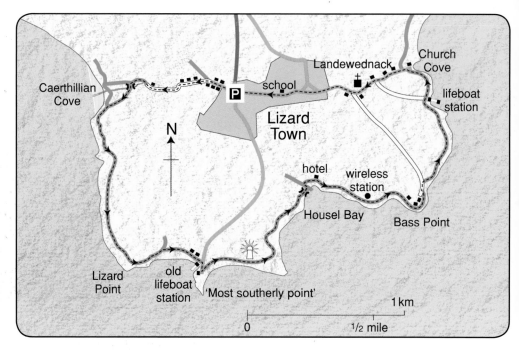

Walk 7 Lizard Point

Distance: 7.3km (4½ miles)   Time: 2¼ hours
Character: The circuit of Lizard Point is one of the most attractive cliff walks in Cornwall. There are over a dozen pedestrian routes out to the coast from Lizard Town, and in my opinion those used here make the best walk. There are a number of ascents and descents, but none are exceptionally strenuous.

Start from the large car park (donations) on which modern Lizard Town is centred. Head westward (past the public conveniences) signed for KYNANCE COVE. Keep left on the main track (PUBLIC BYWAY), which in time becomes a path. Continue past an information board, entering the Lizard (Caerthillian) National Nature Reserve. After about 150m, turn left to cross a stream, then right towards the sea.

At a minor fork either path will bring you to the coast path. Turn left, and climb the steps. Now simply stick to the coast path as it winds, in an appropriately serpentine manner, around to Lizard Point and then to the cluster of cafés and gift shops which make up Britain's 'Most southerly point'.

Turn right onto the access road, pass Britain's most southerly car park and, opposite the National Trust Information Point, turn left

16

along the coast path past the lighthouse and then round to Housel Bay.

The path descends steps, almost to the beach. You might want to take a break at this point, but if not, turn left after crossing the footbridge, then shortly turn right past the Housel Bay Hotel. Keep right, to pass the black-painted wooden huts of the Lizard Wireless Telegraph Station, then Lloyd's Signal Station and the National Coastwatch observation post at Bass Point.

After a short distance on a driveway, bear right onto a path which will lead you to the current lifeboat station. Walk up behind it, then immediately turn right down steps, but just for one flight. Then keep left along the path, which will bring you to Church Cove. Turn left here, up the lane past thatched cottages and the church – at the original heart of the Lizard settlement, called Landewednack. Keep left when the road forks, and continue ahead at the next junction, past the school and Anne's Pasty Shop to the central green.

> The wireless station was erected by Guglielmo Marconi in 1901 to communicate with shipping. Before that time all communication was by flags, using the International (Commercial) Code of Signals – a complex system, which can be found on-line. Lloyd's Signal Station relayed ships' messages by telegraph to London – except in poor visibility.

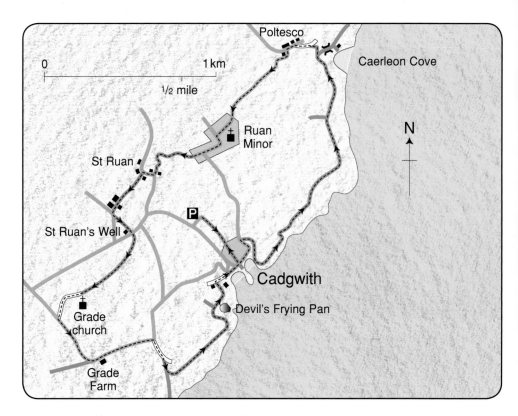

Walk 8 Cadgwith and Poltesco

Distance: 7.6km (4³/₄ miles)   Time: 2 hours
Character: Two lovely stretches of cliff path (the second stretch quite
vertiginous) separated by a pleasant and interesting inland stretch of
footpaths and very quiet lanes. One steep ascent, one steep descent.

Follow the road signs for CADGWITH rather than using a map or
Satnav, and you'll arrive at the village car park. Leave by a footpath at
the lower end which takes you down to the beach. Turn right up the
lane and immediately left out onto the 'Todden' for the classic view of
this most picturesque of Cornwall's villages.

Return to the lane and turn right, past the slipway. Just beyond the
rear of the pub, turn right onto the coast path (acorn sign). Follow
the well-walked path across the cliffs and descend to the next cove,
Poltesco or Caerleon Cove. After a short flight of steps and a footbridge, turn right onto the beach, with its former serpentine factory.

Then return up the steps to the National Trust sign and turn right.
Join a track, then turn left on a lane. After 50m turn left at a lane

junction, passing a watermill then climbing steeply. Keep to the lanes through the village, turning left by the school, then right at the next junction. When the lane turns left at the Methodist church, continue ahead down to a public footpath, which winds to the hamlet of St Ruan.

Turn left at a track junction, then right onto a lane, then after 50 m turn left, PUBLIC FOOTPATH. (You could use the lanes instead, see sketch map.) It emerges onto a field. Climb the field keeping just to the left of the barns.

Reaching a lane, turn left, and shortly bear left (PUBLIC FOOT-PATH) across to St Ruan's Well – still actively in use as a holy place. Walk through the well enclosure and cross the lane ahead, PUBLIC FOOTPATH. Follow the path, aiming just to the left of the church, to a stile, then bear right to pass to the right of Grade church.

Turn left onto a lane and follow it past 'Gwavas Vean'. When it turns left, turn right on a track (PUBLIC FOOTPATH) then bear right onto the signed path. At the next path junction, turn left along the coast path which leads back to Cadgwith via the rim of the Devil's Frying Pan.

On reaching houses, leave by the driveway and turn right down a track (COAST PATH) which becomes a path. On reaching a lane, turn right down the coast path back to the Todden. Turn left past the thatched cottages and retrace your steps to the car park.

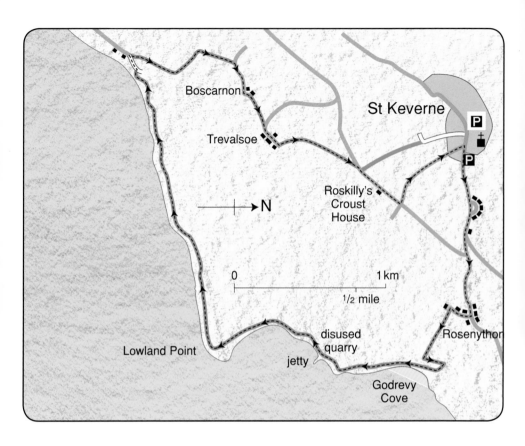

Walk 9 St Keverne

Distance: 8km (5 miles)   Time: 2¹/₄ hours
Character: Coast path and farmland, with a disused quarry and
jetty as a reminder of the Lizard's past industry – and it is a very
recent past. Quiet lanes and footpaths, fairly easy walking throughout.
Roskilly's Croust House is ideally situated for refreshments towards the
end of your walk. Coverack is an alternative starting point: this would
add about 1.4km to the total length of the walk.

Although you can park in St Keverne's main square, it is preferable to
carry on through the square for another 150m to a quieter car park on
the lane to Rosenython (or Rosenithon – the spelling varies).

From that car park, turn left away from the village. At a lane junction, turn right, ROSENITHON. Just past Rosenython farmyard, turn
right onto the coast path. (There is an acorn sign, but it is designed
for walkers coming from the opposite direction!)

20

Just in front of 'Chenhale', turn left onto a footpath. Follow the signed path which makes its way indirectly to the beach. Turn right along the beach then take the coast path at the far end.

Stick to the path as it passes the rusting remains of Dean Quarry. (In 2015, there were plans to reopen the quarry.) It then rounds Lowland Point and you will see Coverack on the far side of the bay.

After passing through rocky outcrops and under a low cliff, the path makes a short steep ascent. Turn left onto an access track. At the top of the slope, turn right (PUBLIC FOOTPATH ST KEVERNE VIA TREVALSOE).

This path climbs gently, with several changes of direction. At a path crossing, turn right. Join a concrete track to Boscarnon, then continue on the path beyond.

Turn right onto a tarmac track into Trevalsoe. At the far end of the hamlet, turn left just before a wall, over a stile. (When I walked it, a gateway was being used instead of the official right-of-way.)

A beaten path then leads over fields and stiles to a lane. You could avoid temptation and continue ahead (FOOTPATH ST KEVERNE). Otherwise, turn right along the lane past Roskilly's Croust House. At a crossroads turn left, ST KEVERNE. On reaching the town centre, turn left for the town square or right for the car park.

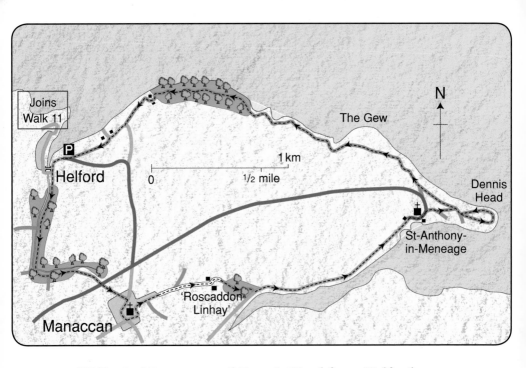

Walk 10   Manaccan and Dennis Head from Helford

Distance: 8.1km (5 miles)   Time: 2¹/₂ hours
Character: Mostly footpaths, some quiet lanes and a lot of woodland
(expect some mud) so very good for a hot day. Beautiful views over
Gillan Creek and Helford River, as well as sea views from Dennis Head.
The walk could be combined with Walk 11, making a full day walk.
By starting from St Anthony-in-Meneage instead of Helford, you could
take refreshment at Helford part way round.

Turn right out of the village car park at Helford (SW 760260). Stay
this side of the creek and continue ahead on PUBLIC FOOTPATH TO
MANACCAN. Ignore side turnings as the path climbs steadily through
woodland. When it emerges, follow the beaten path across a field
to a lane. Cross and take the PUBLIC FOOTPATH, which leads into
Manaccan.

Turn right down a lane, pass the school and then turn left. Walk
through the churchyard, past the decorative Norman doorway of the
little church (unusually there is no porch) and out at the other side.
Continue ahead, signed PUBLIC BRIDLEWAY.

At a fork, keep right, PUBLIC FOOTPATH ST ANTHONY. At 'Roscaddon
Linhay' bear left down a grassy slope, then follow the path through a

small wood. When you reach a lane, turn left and follow it along the creekside to a remarkable little harbour, where St Anthony's church is almost on the beach.

Continue on the lane past the church and uphill, then bear right on a path and turn right (COAST PATH). Beyond the gate, bear left at a fork, slightly uphill. Do not go through the kissing gate at the top, but keep right, then after 100 m turn left through another kissing gate. The path leads out to the headland, with extensive sea views, then round and back to the gate.

Turn right, and this time do turn right through the first kissing gate. Immediately turn left along the hedge. The coast path now leads back towards Helford, winding through woodland and past coves and beaches. Ignore various inland turnings.

After what may seem like a long way, you will pass behind a house and shortly afterwards arrive at a lane. Keep right, COAST PATH HELFORD. As the lane swings right, passing a house, turn left (COAST PATH TO VILLAGE) – do not go into the garden ahead of you, but sharp left up a short flight of steps. This path leads back to the car park.

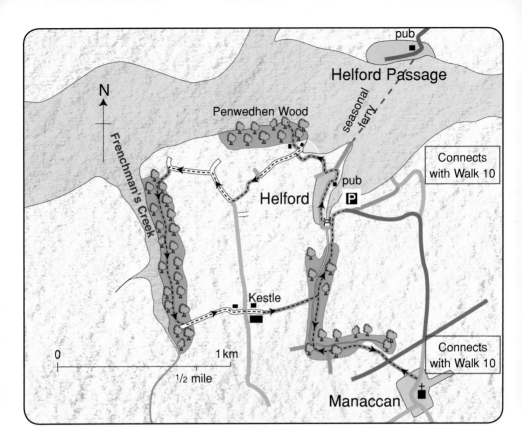

Walk 11 Frenchman's Creek

Distance: Basic circuit 5.3km (3¹/₄ miles)   Time: 1¹/₄ hours
Character: Almost entirely on footpaths, with views over the Helford
River and woodland beside the famous creek. It can be extended by a
short foray to Penwedhen Wood, or by a there-and-back diversion to
Manaccan village, making it approximately 7.5km in total. It can also
be combined with Walk 10, making a walk of nearly 12km.

Turn right out of the Helford village car park (SW760260) down to
the creek. Turn right over the footbridge, then right again. Walk past
the village shop and the Shipwright's Arms. At a junction, turn right if
you want to visit the ferry pier; otherwise turn sharp left up a concrete
track. After 100m turn right, PUBLIC FOOTPATH.

Cross the back of Penarvon Cove. If you want to explore the very
quiet woodland of Penwedhen, turn right, then just before 'Penguin'
turn sharp left up steps, cross a yard and go straight ahead to a kissing
gate into the woodland.

24

Otherwise, turn left up the track, FRENCHMAN'S CREEK. Join a tarmac drive and continue uphill to a T-junction. Turn right, FRENCHMAN'S CREEK PERMISSIVE PATH. At the next track junction, turn left. Near the foot of the slope, turn left onto a footpath, FRENCHMAN'S CREEK (PERMISSIVE). This leads down to the creek.

In summer the vegetation is so lush that you get only a few tantalising glimpses of the water – or mud: plenty of opportunity here to hide a pirate vessel or two!

At the head of the creek the path bears left uphill. Turn left on a track and climb to a lane. Cross over and continue through Kestle, then with the hedge on your left descend to enter woodland.

To return to the village, turn left and follow the path down beside the stream.

To extend the walk to Manaccan, or to connect with Walk 10, turn right. Follow the main path, ignoring side turnings. When the path leaves the wood, follow it over a field to a lane. Cross and continue (PUBLIC FOOTPATH) into Manaccan.

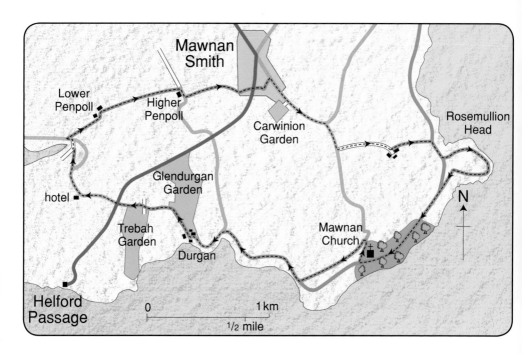

Walk 12 Durgan and Rosemullion Head

Distance: 8.5km (5¼ miles)   Time: 2¼ hours
*Character: Some lovely coastline, passing gardens open to the public
so you could combine the walk with one or more visits. The coastal
path involves some uneven walking, and some parts of the walk can
be very muddy – best avoided after heavy rain. The lanes used can
become fairly busy in summer.*

Start from the car park by Mawnan church or from nearby roadside
parking (donation requested). Facing the church, leave by a pedestrian gate on your right and walk downhill. Go between gateposts
and continue beside a stream down to a beach. Turn right along the
coast path.

Keep to the coastal path at junctions, then join the lane and go down
to Durgan. Turn right, and either visit Glendurgan (there's a gate to
the right) or keep left on the track uphill, signed GARDEN ENTRANCE.
Then at the garden entrance continue uphill past the signpost.

Join a track and pass the entrance to Trebah Gardens, continuing
on a rough track, then along a lane (PORT NAVAS). Keep right at the
entrance to Budock Vean, and descend the lane with care, then bear
left (PUBLIC FOOTPATH).

26

Cut diagonally down the field and leave by a kissing gate on your left. Turn right down the lane, then turn left at the bottom, and after 20m sharp right up a farm track. Follow the track as it curves left into Lower Penpoll farm, then turn right following the white painted arrows, and out along a track, then through fields and continue ahead.

At the hamlet of Higher Penpoll, turn right down the lane then after 100m turn left (PUBLIC FOOTPATH).

Ultimately you cross a brook. Continue through a gateway and head diagonally right up the field to a stile about 100m down from the top corner on the far side. A path then leads to a road. (Mawnan Smith, with its pub, café and shops, is to your left.) Cross the road and take the path through to another road. Turn right up the road, passing Carwinion Garden, no longer open to the public at the time of printing. At a lane junction, turn right (OLD CHURCH ROAD).

After 200m, turn left FOOTPATH ONLY TO ROSEMULLION HEAD. It leads to a farm: just inside the gate, turn left (COAST PATH) and head out to the coast path. Turn right. At a gateway, continue ahead if you want to miss Rosemullion Head, saving perhaps 500m, or take the path down to the left and follow it around the headland.

Either way, you'll continue on the coastal path into scrub and then a wood. At the top of the wood, a kissing gate leads to a bench with a lovely view. From the bench, retrace your steps for 30m and bear left at a fork in the path, which will take you back to the church car park.

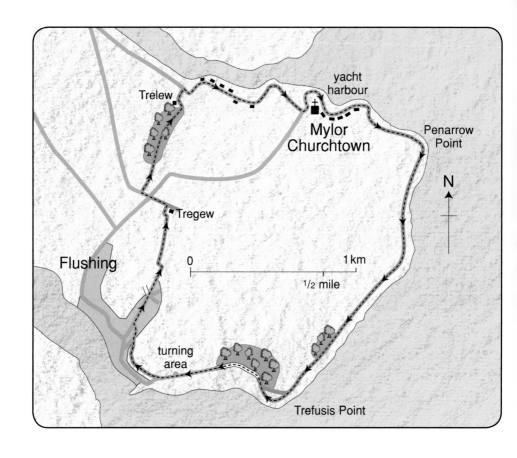

Walk 13 Flushing and Mylor Churchtown

Distance: 6.6km (4 miles)   Time: 1 3/4 hours
Character: An easy walk, starting with a pleasant inland stretch, then
a visit to the yachting centre at Mylor, completed by a gentle stroll to
Trefusis Point, with extensive views over Carrick Roads and Falmouth
docks and town.

Park on the road between Flushing and Trefusis Point – there is usually space beyond the turning point. Walk back towards Flushing.
When the road dips away to the left, continue ahead up a slope,
PUBLIC FOOTPATH. Go through the park. After descending steps,
turn left, then right along a street. At a T-junction by the Methodist
church, turn right and follow the street uphill.

Opposite KERSEY CLOSE, when the street bears right, take the PUBLIC
FOOTPATH almost straight ahead. At first it's enclosed, then keep the

field hedge on your left. Just before a house, turn left over a stile, which shortly brings you to a tarmac track. Turn left along it.

Cross the road ahead and after 60 m turn right, PUBLIC FOOTPATH TRELEW. Follow this path through a field, then a wood, and finally right along a driveway to a lane.

Turn right along the lane, which snakes around, then runs parallel to the creek. When it ends, continue on a footpath. Cross a lane to visit Mylor church. There is no right of way through the attactive churchyard, so return to the lane and follow it down and round past the yacht harbour.

Beyond the harbour, continue along the PRIVATE ROAD ACCESS ONLY, which is also a public footpath. Soon after it becomes a track, take the footpath which bears off to the left and follows the shore. The views soon open out, and continue till you round Trefusis Point.

Ultimately the path arrives at a gate, beyond which a track leads to the road in which you parked.

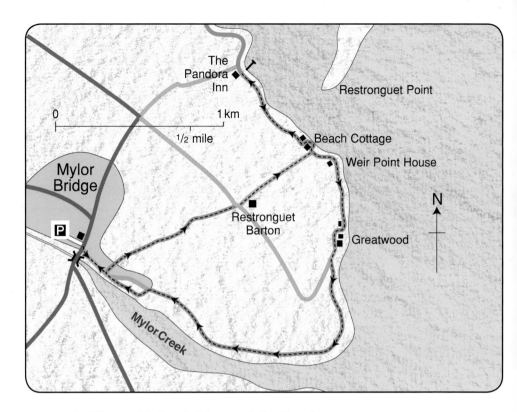

Walk 14 Mylor Bridge and the Pandora

Distance: 6km (3³/₄ miles)   Time: 1³/₄ hours
Character: A very easy, shady, walk with lovely views over Carrick
Roads and Mylor Creek, and as its destination the famous Pandora Inn
– where parking is very limited, so this is a good way to avoid fustration!

Park in the free car park at Mylor Bridge (just below the pub car park). Leaving the car park, cross the main street and bear right down TREVELLAN ROAD. At the far end of the quay, turn left, PUBLIC FOOTPATH – *not* the path to Restronguet and Greatwood.

This path soon becomes a shady, tunnel-like holloway and leads steadily up to a lane junction. Continue ahead, signed WEIR, and pass Restronguet Barton. When you reach the estuary, turn left along the beach, then inland behind 'Beach Cottage'. Paths and tracks lead to the Pandora Inn.

Now retrace your steps to the beach. Rather than going back up the lane, turn left, PUBLIC FOOTPATH GREATWOOD, keeping left at the fork and then branching left on an enclosed path at Weir Point House.

Immediately beyond a terrace of cottages, turn right to pass above Greatwood House. Join a tarmac track then after 100m turn left down a track, which soon curves to the right.

This path leads along the coast, through woodland and fields, before turning up the side of Mylor Creek, finally crossing a field to reach the village at TREVELLAN ROAD. Immediately turn left down a footpath, which runs behind the back gardens, arriving at the quay. Retrace your steps to the car park.

The Pandora Inn

The inn's original function is indicated by its ancient name, the 'Passage House', where travellers on the old road between Penryn and Truro could await the ferry: this ran from at least the 15th century until about 1960. The inn later became 'The Ship' and by 1871 was known as the 'Pandora' – named after the ship sent to Tahiti to arrest the mutineers from HMS *Bounty*. Quays were built here in the late 18th century so that machinery from Perran Foundry could be transferred from barges to ocean-going ships.

Some other Bossiney books about Cornwall

Cornish ports and harbours, Ian Heard
Ian Heard is an artist who grew up in a boatyard at Mylor, with an intuitive sense of the sea and an appreciation of Cornwall's magnificent coastline. This book contains paintings of Porthleven, Mullion Cove, Cadgwith, Coverack and Gweek, among many other places.

About St Michael's Mount, Michael Sagar-Fenton
The author explores the remarkable history of this magical island, as a monastery, as a fortress and as a country house, now administered by The National Trust.

Bossiney walks books
Bossiney Books publishes walks books covering the whole of Cornwall and Devon and much of Somerset.
Our 'shortish walks' books contain walks typically of 6-8 km, and 'really short walks' are 3-5 km.

For Cornwall we have:
Shortish walks near the Land's End
Shortish walks – Truro to Looe
Shortish walk – St Ives to Padstow
Shortish walks – Bodmin Moor
Shortish walks in north Cornwall
Really short walks in north Cornwall